Great GREETING CARD Crafts

By Muriel Hemmings

STANDARD
PUBLISHING
Cincinnati, Ohio

FRONT COVER:

Illustrated by Dan Farris
Edited by Karen Brewer

The Standard Publishing Company, Cincinnati, Ohio
A division of Standex International Corporation

01 00 99 98 97 96 95 94   5 4 3 2 1

ISBN 0-7847-0147-4

Read Me First!

Greeting cards are beautiful but costly. This book recycles those beautiful cards into great one-of-a-kind crafts!

Use a memorable card to make a craft to preserve for a lifetime. Send a card from a friend back to your friend as a special treat. Or simply use those cards that you normally throw away to create some fun.

These crafts are suitable for all ages. Children will enjoy them as well as senior citizens. Families can make crafts together for special occasions, gifts, or play.

The key to *Great Greeting Card Crafts* is the selection of the cards. Each project will be unique because each card is different. Select cards according to their design, paper weight, and size. You may want to test a difficult project on a scrap card before using your favorite card.

As a rule, only card fronts are used for crafts. If the back is needed, directions will explain. Patterns are provided that can be sized larger or smaller in a copy machine.

89156

Contents

Beads

Fun Things for Kids

Christmas

● Easy

▲ Moderately Easy

■ Requires Some Help

★ Requires Good Dexterity

Gifts to Make

Hanging Hearts
(Pictured on cover.)

1. Cut two cards into heart shapes.

2. Lay hearts face down. Apply glue to the edge of each heart and glue lace around edges.

3. Cut a piece of ribbon about 7" long. Glue one end of the ribbon to the back of one heart and the other end of the ribbon to the other heart.

4. For added decoration, glue a 1" piece of ribbon on the back of each heart so the end shows above the top.

Hang hearts on a wooden peg or over the back of a wooden chair.

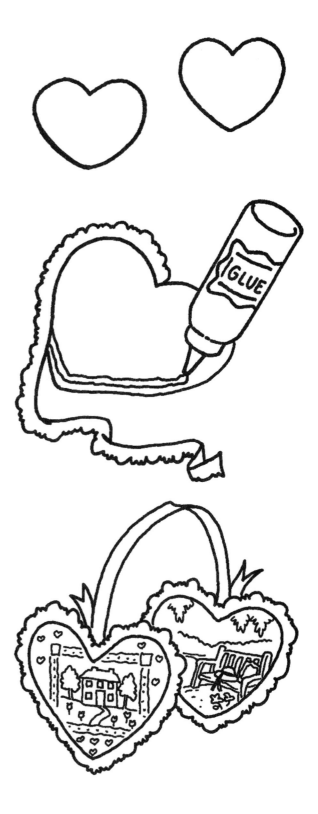

Recipe Box
(Pictured on cover.)

1. Cut two card fronts to be 5⅛" by 5".

2. Fold each with right sides out as in the diagram.

3. Glue the 2" sections on top of each other to form a double thickness.

4. Cut two pieces of card to be 2" by 5".

5. Fold each with right sides out as in the diagram.

6. Glue the 2" sections to the bottom to complete the four sides.

7. Tape the corners on the inside to hold the box together.

8. Glue a wide ribbon around the outside for decoration and to give the box added strength. Add card cutouts for decoration.

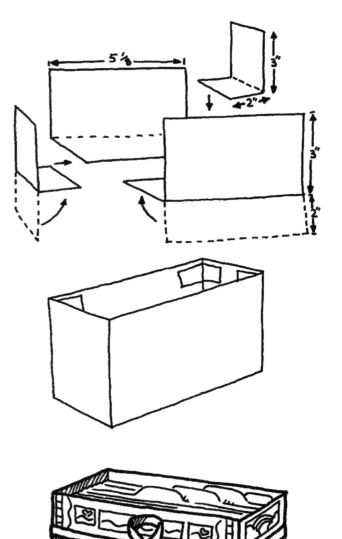

Insert recipe cards.
Write a favorite recipe on one card to make the gift extra special!

Note Pad Covers

One Kind

1. Slip a small note pad inside a card and cut the card to the same size. Be sure enough room is allowed at the card fold to wrap around the binding of the pad.

2. Open the card and apply glue to both the inside front, fold, and inside back.

3. Insert the pad so that the pad's front and back cover are glued to the card.

Another Kind

1. Cut two cards to the size of loose note paper.

2. Punch three holes down one side of all the pieces.

3. Stack all pieces with holes aligned and a cover piece on the bottom and top.

4. Thread yarn up hole A and down hole C.

5. Then thread both ends of the yarn up through hole B.

6. Knot yarn and tie in a bow.

*Let love and faithfulness
never leave you; . . .
Write them on the tablet of your heart*
(Proverbs 3:3).

A Basket

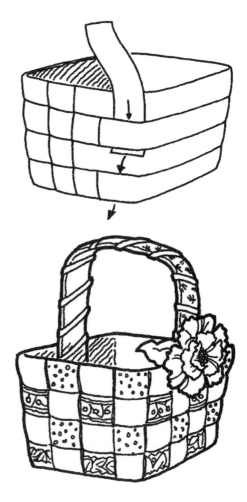

1. Begin with a plastic fruit or vegetable basket.

2. Cut strips of cards to weave through the basket sides. Alternate a patterned strip with a plain strip for an interesting design.

3. Use a card strip to glue on as a handle.

4. Add other decorations such as silk flowers and ribbon if desired.

Fill the basket with goodies and take it to a shut-in!

Hanging Decoration

1. Cut a wide piece of lace into a six to eight inch strip.

2. Cut several shapes from cards.

3. Glue the shapes down the lace strip.

4. Glue ribbon to the top back to make a hanger or weave cord into the lace.

Hang these decorations on wooden pegs or a doorknob.

Woven Heart

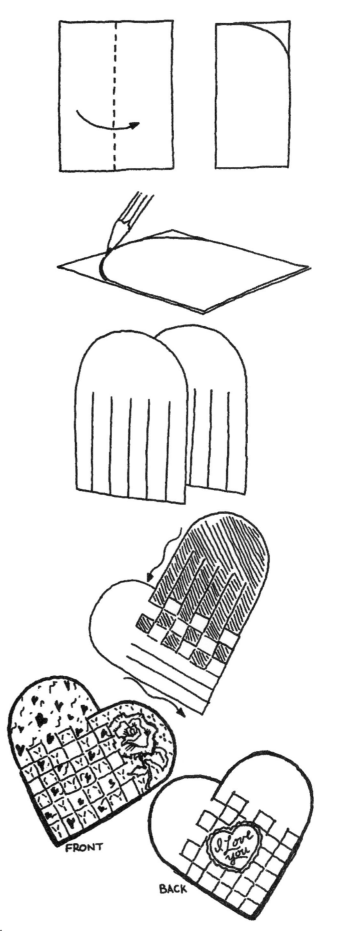

1. Choose two cards similar in size but contrasted in color and design.

2. Fold one card in half and cut as illustrated.

3. Open and trace onto the other card and cut to match.

4. Cut five slits in each card from the bottom straight edge about three fourths up.

5. Place the cards so the curved tops resemble a heart. Weave the strips together for a special valentine.

6. Add a gummed label or glue a small paper heart to the back, and write a message.

*Serve the Lord your God
with all your heart
and with all your soul*
(Deuteronomy 10:12).

FRONT

BACK

Picture Frame

1. Start by trimming a card into a square. Fold it in half from both directions to find the center.

2. Open the square and fold each of the four corners to meet at the center point.

3. Fold each corner at the center, back to the folded edge.

4. Glue or tape a photo in the square left in the center. Or insert a verse from another card.

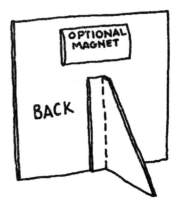

5. Add a strip of magnetic tape to the back and hang your photo and frame on the refrigerator. Or glue two plain card pieces together to make a sturdy stand. Cut the double thickness into a wedge as illustrated. Fold and glue to the back of the frame so that it stands.

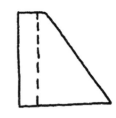

*Make a picture frame
for Mother's Day.*

Bookmarks

(Pictured on cover.)

1. Cut a card lengthwise into three or four strips. (Pinking shears add an interesting effect.)

2. Trim the top and bottom edges of each strip as desired.

3. Punch a hole in one end of each.

4. Use ribbon, yarn, or cord to tie into the hole of each.

*Add a favorite Bible verse
or a greeting to a friend
on the back!*

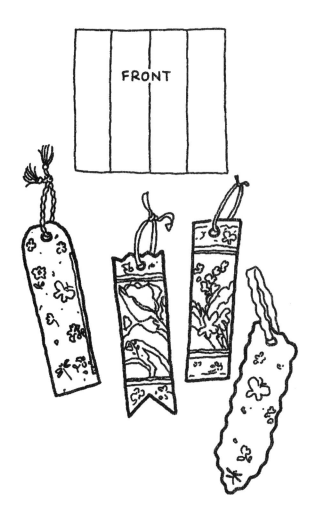

Desk Organizer

1. Choose a large sturdy card for a base. Glue the front to the back for double thickness.

2. Choose several sturdy cards to roll into cylinders of various heights and diameters.

3. Glue cylinders (decorated side out) to the base (decorated side up) and to each other.

*Fill cylinders with pens, paper clips,
rubber bands, coins, thumb tacks, etc.*

Brooch
(Pictured on cover.)

1. Cut out flowers and leaves from cards.

2. Stack flowers. Glue just the centers of flowers and the ends of leaves into an arrangement.

3. Bend ends up to make the arrangement three dimensional.

4. Coat with a clear gloss spray or clear nail polish. Dry thoroughly.

5. Glue a metal pin fastener on the back.

Grandmothers will love these!

BACK

Gift Box

(Pictured on cover.)

1. Separate the front from the back of a card.

2. Trim the back of the card about ⅟₁₆" on one horizontal side and one vertical side.

3. On the wrong sides of each piece, draw a line one inch from all sides as illustrated.

4. Fold on these lines and snip corners as illustrated.

5. Glue corners inside end flaps to create a box bottom and a box lid.

*Hide something special
inside your gift box!*

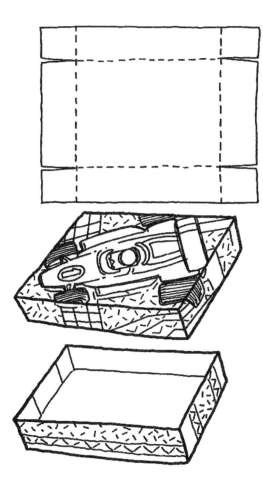

Gift Tags

1. Choose a card that is plain on the inside front cover.

2. Cut it into about four strips. (Use pinking sheers for added design.)

3. Fold each strip in half. Punch a hole near the fold.

4. Cut a six inch piece of ribbon or yarn and fold it in half. Insert the loop through the hole and insert the ends through the loop.

5. Tie the tag to your gift.

*God loves a cheerful giver
(2 Corinthians 9:7).*

Secret Message Card

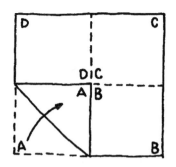

1. Trim a card into a square.

2. With the design face down, fold the square in half twice to find the center. Then open the card.

3. Fold each of the four corners of the square to meet at the center point.

4. Open the card and write a secret message.

5. Close the card with a small piece of tape.

A gift given in secret soothes anger (Proverbs 21:14).

Pop-Up Cards

One Kind

1. Find two cards and trim them to the same size.

2. Turn one card inside out.

3. Cut two slits in it (about ½" apart) from the fold to about the center. (The illustration shows two pairs of slits.)

4. Pull the section between the two slits to the inside of the card to make the pop-up base.

5. Cut out an interesting picture from another card. Glue one half of the picture to the left of the fold on the pop-up base. Let one half of the picture hang to the right of the fold unglued.

6. Other pictures can be cut out to decorate the edges inside the card. (Try using paper springs as described on page 28 to mount some springing pictures.)

7. Glue the other card to the back of the pop-up card to cover the holes created by the pop-up base.

*To make an even more interesting pop-up card,
cut four or six slits and glue in two or three pictures.
Try varying the length of each pair of slits for another interesting effect.*

Another Kind

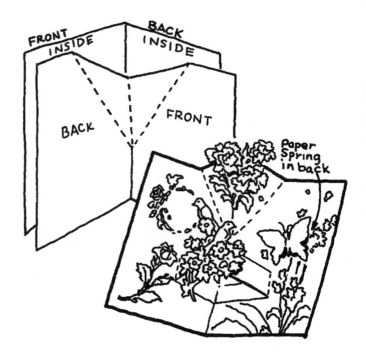

1. Find two cards and trim them to the same size.

2. Turn one card inside out and turn the top fold down making a pop-up triangle.

3. Cut out pictures from other cards to glue on the pop-up triangle.

4. Decorate the inside of the card with other cutouts, or glue objects on paper springs to the inside. (See page 28 for instructions for paper springs.)

5. Glue the other card to the back of the pop-up card.

Try a combination of both pop-up cards.
Put a pop-up triangle at the top and a pop-up base at the bottom.

Decorate for a Party

Treat Holder
(Pictured on cover.)

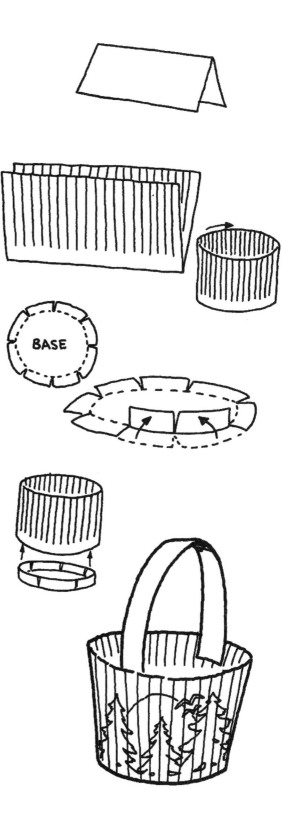

1. Fold a rectangular card lengthwise.

2. Cut the card into narrow strips not quite to the fold.

3. Bring ends together to make a circle. Tape ends together.

4. Cut a plain circle a little bit bigger than the circumference of the holder.

5. Snip the edge of the circle about every half inch and fold up the tabs.

6. Glue or tape the circle bottom to the holder by inserting the folded tabs into the bottom of the holder.

7. Add a handle made from a narrow strip of card.

Fill with nuts and mints!

Candle Decoration
(Pictured on cover.)

1. Cut a thin card to approximately 4" x 5".

2. Place the card face down. Fold the two 5" sides in to the center like the diagram.

3. Place a small piece of tape at each end to keep the card folded.

4. Cut the card into narrow strips from both folded sides down to about the width of the tape.

5. Wrap into a circle and tape.

6. Bend slightly into an hour glass shape.

7. Set the decoration over a taper candle for a festive touch.

Make a pair!

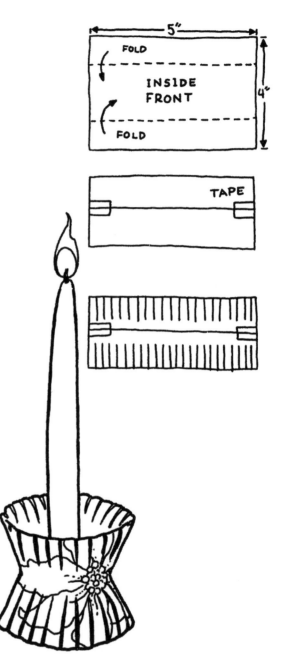

Napkin Holder

1. Trim four cards to approximately 5" x 6". Glue them into pairs with wrong sides together for sturdy double thickness.

2. Scallop one 6" edge on each card.

3. Fold each as in the diagram.

4. Glue the two pieces together to form four thicknesses as shown.

Fill with paper napkins.

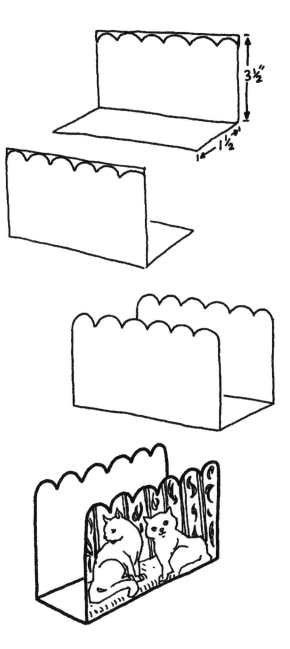

A Flower

1. Cut off about ¼ of the card front (A).

2. Cut the small card piece (A) into small strips leaving one side intact.

3. Roll the strip tightly and tape the bottom edge securely. This is the flower's stamen.

4. Fold the large rectangle (B) in half lengthwise.

5. Cut as shown, leaving the folded side intact. This is the flower's petals.

6. Assemble the flower by taping a chenille wire to the stamen.

7. Then wrap the petals around the stamen and wire with the decorative side out. Tape or glue securely at the base of the flower.

8. Add leaves cut from cards or cut a leaf shape from any green card.

9. Optional: Wrap the stem wire with floral tape.

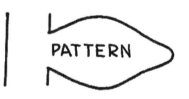

PATTERN

Flowers appear on the earth;
the season of singing has come
(Song of Solomon 2:12).

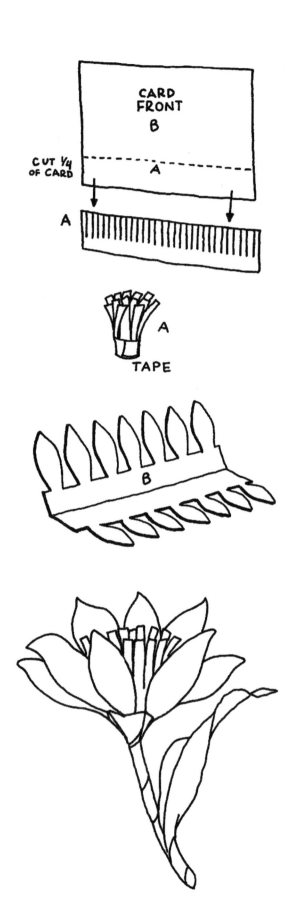

Place Cards

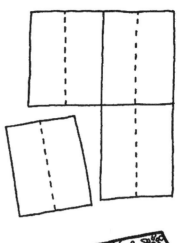

1. Cut a card into four rectangles as shown.

2. Fold each in half so cards will stand like a tent.

3. Add each guest's name to a card.

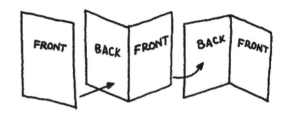

*Use holiday cards
to add a special touch to holiday parties!*

Display Background

1. Choose as many cards as you wish that have a similar theme or tell a story such as Christmas cards. Put the cards in order. Do not trim off the backs, but trim all cards to the same size.

2. Cut the back off only the first card in the series.

3. Glue the first card (without a back) over the back of the second card. Glue the front of the second card over the back of the third card. Continue until all cards are glued together.

*Set the cards up as a background
for a crèche, a birthday cake,
or any theme.*

Mobiles

Basic Mobile

1. Cut two cards into identical circles about 4-6 inches in diameter.

2. Glue circles together with wrong sides together.

3. Punch about twelve holes evenly around the edge. This will be the top of the mobile.

4. Choose two small pictures (from cards) for each hole. Cut each pair of shapes identically with pictures facing out.

5. Glue each pair together.

6. Punch a hole in each pair and tie the end of about two feet of dark thread to each hole.

7. Tie the other end of each string around a hole in the mobile top, leaving several inches of thread at the top. Vary lengths of hanging pairs to make the mobile interesting.

8. Hold the mobile top parallel to your work table and gather all the loose threads at the top. Tie in a loop so that the mobile top hangs evenly.

A Quick Mobile

1. Cut a large card into a circle.

2. Cut the circle into one continuous thin strip as diagrammed.

3. Tug on each end to make a spring.

4. Punch a hole in one end and add a thread loop for hanging.

5. Cut two shapes from cards. Glue one to the top and one to the bottom for decoration.

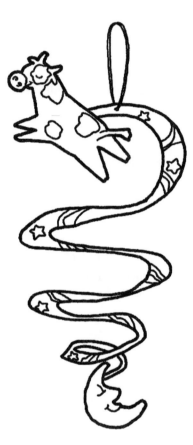

Bird Mobile

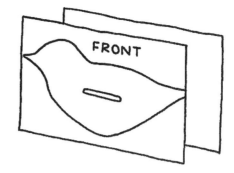

1. Use two card fronts with wrong sides together and the pattern below to trace and cut out a bird body.

2. Glue the two pieces of the bird body together, but leave the tail open.

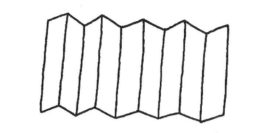

3. Use a thin card for the tail. Pleat the shorter side from end to end.

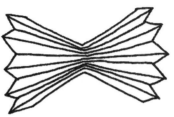

4. Cut a horizontal slit in the bird's body. Insert the pleated card as wings.

5. Pleat another thin card and glue one end into the tail opening.

6. Glue on two rhinestones or studs for eyes.

7. Punch a hole in the bird's back and tie a long dark thread into the hole to hang the bird.

Try making several birds to string onto a basic mobile (see page 25).

PATTERN

Paper Spring Mobile

1. Cut several colorful cards into ¾" wide strips.

   Note: Strips can be made longer by gluing or taping strips together.

2. Tape or glue two equal length strips at right angles.

3. Alternate folding one over the other until all the paper is folded.

4. Tape or glue the ends.

5. Cut two cards into identical circles about 4-6 inches in diameter. This will be the top of the mobile.

6. Glue circles together with wrong sides together.

7. Punch holes evenly around the circle edge—one for each spring to be hung.

8. Punch a hole in one end of each spring and tie in one end of a two foot dark thread.

9. Tie each string around a hole in the mobile top, leaving several inches of thread at the top. Vary lengths of hanging thread.

10. Hold the mobile top parallel to your work table, and gather all loose threads at the top. Tie in a loop so that the mobile top hangs evenly.

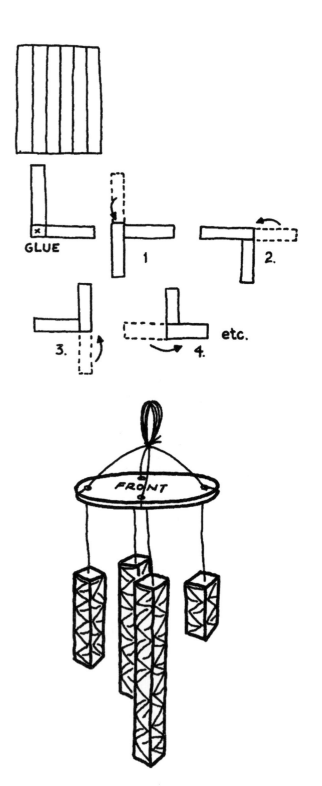

Mosaics

Serving Tray
(Pictured on cover.)

1. Snip several colorful cards into multi-shaped pieces.

2. Cover the top of a foam meat tray with glue and overlapping multi-shaped card pieces.

3. Cut a clear piece of Con-Tact® paper to be about one inch larger than the tray on all sides.

4. Cover the mosaic with the clear Con-Tact® paper and fold the edges to the underside of the tray. Cutting slits at each corner of the Con-Tact® paper will help it fold under more easily.

Serve cookies on your tray to a friend.

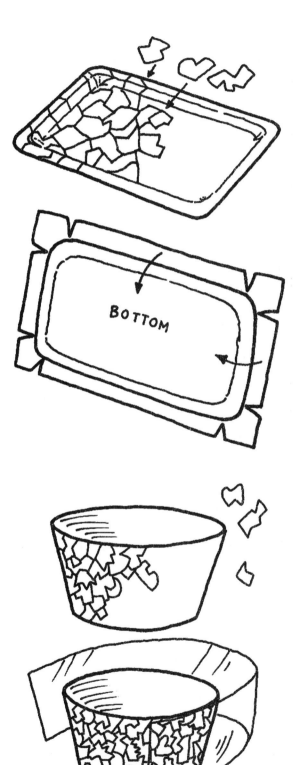

Planter

1. Snip several colorful cards into multi-shaped pieces.

2. Cover the outside of a margarine tub with glue and overlapping multi-shaped card pieces. (It is not necessary to cover the bottom.)

3. Cut a strip of clear Con-Tact® paper slightly larger than the width of the tub. Cover the mosaic with the Con-Tact® paper. Trim paper edges.

Insert a potted plant, or use this container to hold treasures.

Bookends or Doorstop

1. Snip several colorful cards into multi-shaped pieces.

2. Completely cover one or two clean bricks with glue and overlapping multi-shaped card pieces.

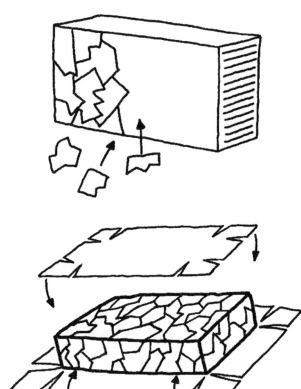

3. Lay the brick horizontally on its widest side on top of a piece of clear Con-Tact® paper. Cut the paper large enough to fold the sides two-thirds up each side of the brick. Cut two pieces the same size.

4. Cover the mosaic on one side of the brick and fold the edges up the sides. Cutting slits at each corner of the Con-Tact® paper will help it fold more easily. Then cover the other side and fold over the edges. Con-Tact® paper on the sides of the brick will over lap, covering the whole brick securely.

Flower Vase

1. Snip several colorful cards into multi-shaped pieces.

2. Cover the outside of a juice can with glue and overlapping multi-shaped card pieces.

3. Cut a strip of clear contact paper the height of the can. Apply the contact paper over the mosaic.

4. Cut flowers from other cards and glue them to twigs.

5. Fill the vase with pebbles or sand and stand the "flowers" in your flower vase.

Decorate banquet tables with these flower vases.

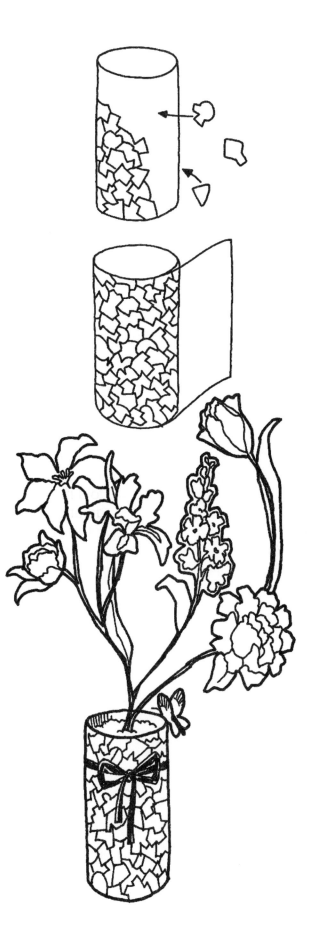

Beads

Basic Card Beads

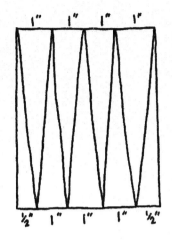

1. Turn a colorful card face down.

2. Rule and cut a card into long triangles measuring an inch wide at the broadest end. See diagram. (Throw away ½" strips.)

3. Use a nail to roll the triangles decorated side out and starting at the widest end.

4. Apply glue to the triangle tip and secure to form an oval shaped bead.

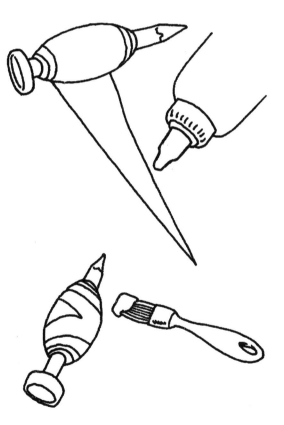

5. Slide the bead off the nail and hold for a few seconds to make sure it is secure. (Beads may be clamped with clothespins to dry.)

6. Beads will be prettier and last longer if brushed or sprayed with clear gloss.

Use these beads for a variety of projects on the following pages.

Bead Doll

Number of beads needed:
    9 card beads
    1 20mm wood bead

1. Start with a 5" piece of chenille wire
    and a 7" piece.

2. Fold the 7" wire in half. Add a drop of
    glue on the fold and insert it into the
    wood bead. These are the legs.

3. Wrap the 5" wire around the neck, just
    below the head, and as tightly as
    possible. These are the arms.

4. Place two card beads on each arm and
    bend the wire ends to form hands.

5. Push one card bead onto both legs for
    a body. Then place two card beads on
    each leg and bend the wire ends to
    form the feet.

6. Add yarn hair and draw a face as
    desired.

*Your doll can bend its knees and elbows
and turn its head. Sit the doll on the edge
of a flower pot, or make it climb up a plant.
It will stand by itself if feet are glued to a
stiff square card.*

34

Bead Flower
(Pictured on cover.)

Number of beads needed:
   5 card beads
   6 6mm round plastic beads

1. Begin with a 14" thin flexible wire.

2. Slip one end of the wire up through a card bead then through a small plastic bead and back down the card bead.

3. Leave one end of the wire about 3" long. Twist the two ends of wire together at the bottom of the card bead.

4. Use the long wire to repeat step two. Twist the two wires at the bottom of the second card bead.

5. Continue repeating step two to string all beads.

6. Add a plastic bead at the end for a flower center. Twist the two wire ends securely to form a stem.

7. Optional: Cover the stem wires with floral tape. Add a silk leaf.

Use flowers in a small bud vase,
make a corsage,
or add one to a package for decoration.

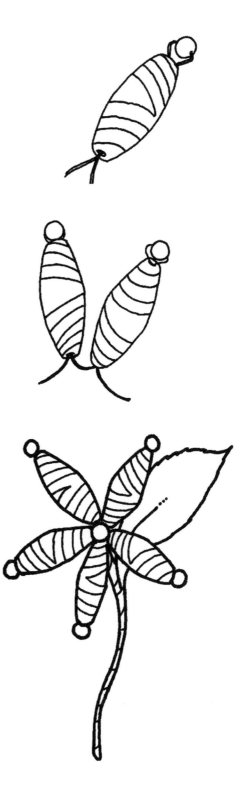

35

Bead Basket

Number of beads needed:
    106 card beads
    85 8mm round plastic beads

1. Place 100 card beads on 100 inch long
    (not measuring the head) safety pins.

2. ROW ONE

    a. Use a 12" wire to string 20 plastic
        beads and 20 card beads in this
        order: pin head, plastic bead, pen
        head, plastic bead, etc.

    b. Join the two wire ends to form a
        circle and twist tightly with pliers.
        Cut off ends.

    Note: Be sure that all bare safety pin
    sides are facing *inside* the circle.

3. ROW TWO

    a. Use a 12" wire to add new beads to
        row one. String in this order: row
        one pin tail, new pin tail, row one
        pin tail, new pin tail, etc.

    b. Join the two wire ends to form a
        circle and twist tightly with pliers.
        Cut off ends.

    Note: Be sure that all bare safety pin
    sides are facing *inside* the circle.

4. ROW THREE

    a. Use an 18" wire to add new beads
        to row two. String in this order: new
        pin tail, row two pin head, new pin
        tail, row two pin head, etc.

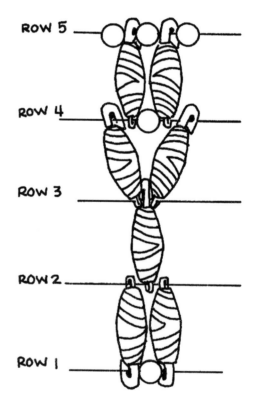

ROW 5

ROW 4

ROW 3

ROW 2

ROW 1

b. Join the two wire ends to form a circle and twist tightly with pliers. Cut off ends.

Note: Be sure all new bare safety pin sides are facing *outside* the circle.

5. ROW FOUR

a. Use a 24" wire to add new beads to row three. String in this order: row three pin head, new pin tail, new plastic bead, new pin tail, row three pin head, new pin tail, new plastic bead, new pin tail, etc.

b. Join the two wire ends to form a circle and twist tightly with pliers. Cut off.

Note: Be sure all new bare safety pin sides are facing *outside* the circle.

6. ROW FIVE

a. Use a 24" wire to add new beads to row four. String in this order: new plastic bead, row four pin head, new plastic bead, row four pin head, new plastic bead, etc.

b. Join the two wire ends to form a circle. Twist tightly with pliers. Cut off ends.

7. HANDLE

a. Use a 12" wire to string six card beads alternately with five round beads.

b. Twist each wire end around the top of the basket. Cut off ends.

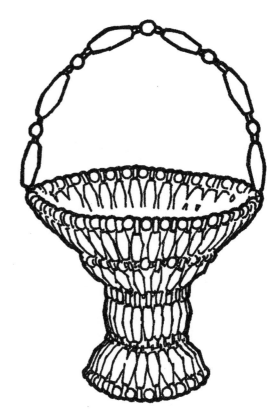

The Acrobat

Number of beads needed:
  9 card beads
  5 8mm round plastic beads
  1 20mm wood bead

1. Draw a face on the wood bead.

2. Measure and cut a piece of heavy thread two feet long.

3. String onto the thread:
   a. one plastic bead,
   b. wood bead, and
   c. a small two-hole button.

4. Leaving a two inch loop, return the thread through:
   a. the button,
   b. wood bead, and
   c. the plastic bead.

5. Tie a knot at A and B.

6. Use one end of the thread and string on:
   a. two card beads and
   b. one plastic bead.

   Then return the thread through the two card beads.

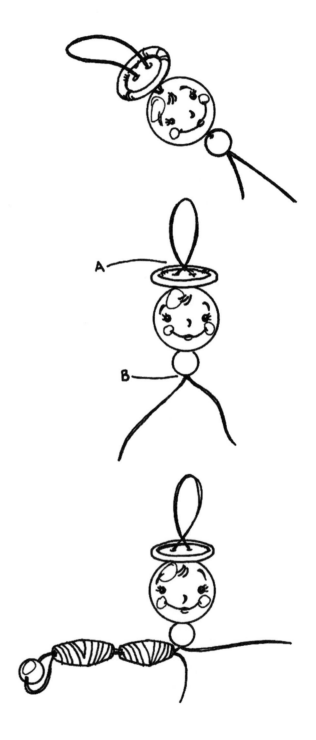

7. Repeat step 6 for the other end of the thread.

8. Tie a knot at C.

9. String one card bead on both threads for the body.

10. Use one end of the thread, and string on:
    a. two card beads and
    b. one plastic bead.

    Then return the thread through the two card beads.

11. Repeat step 10 for the other end of the thread.

12. Tie the two thread ends together at D and trim.

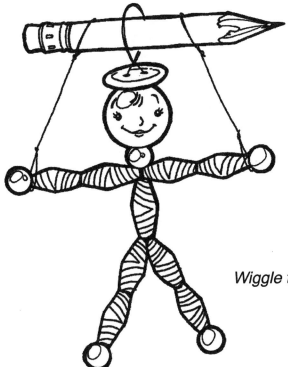

Slip a pencil through the top loop.
Tie the arms to the pencil too.
Wiggle the pencil, and watch the acrobat perform!

Bead Vase or Container

Number of beads needed:
    48 card beads
    48 8mm round plastic beads
    48 6mm round plastic beads

Note: Be sure that all bare safety pin sides are always facing inside the circle.

1. Place 48 card beads on 48 inch long (not measuring the head) safety pins.

2. ROW ONE

    a. Use a 16" wire to string 24 8mm beads alternately with 24 safety pin heads.

    b. Join the two wire ends to form a circle and twist tightly with pliers. Cut off ends.

3. ROW TWO

    a. Use a 16" wire to add new beads to row one. String in this order: row one pin tail, new 6mm plastic bead, new pin head, new 6mm plastic bead, row one pin tail, new 6mm plastic bead, new pin head, new 6mm plastic bead, etc.

    b. Join the two wire ends to form a circle and twist tightly with pliers. Cut off ends.

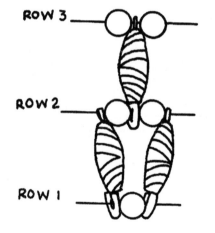

4. ROW THREE

   a. Use a 16" wire to add new beads to row two. String in this order: new 8mm plastic bead, row two pin tail, new 8mm plastic bead, row two pin tail, etc.

   b. Join the two wire ends to form a circle and twist tightly with pliers. Cut off ends.

5. Stretch three wires diagonally across the bottom and twist tightly around wire edge. Cut off ends.

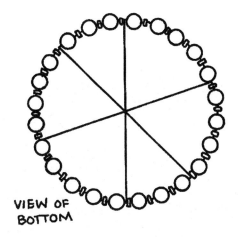

VIEW OF BOTTOM

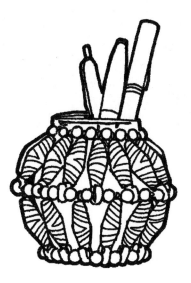

Place a baby food jar inside and fill the container with a plant, pencils, carrot sticks, or anything!

41

Bead Necklace and Bracelet

Number of beads needed: As desired

1. Cut a piece of elastic cord to the desired length.

2. String card beads alternated with plastic beads or pearls.

3. Tie cord ends together to form a necklace or bracelet.

Fun Things for Kids

Catch the Ball
(Pictured on cover.)

1. Cut a colorful card into a square. The sides of the square should measure at least 4½ inches.

2. Make a triangle by folding A to D with wrong sides together.

3. Fold corner B to point E.

4. Fold corner F to point C.

5. Open corners at D and fold each down so that the wrong side shows.

6. Hold and squeeze at the corners to make an open cup.

7. Tape one end of a 12 inch string into the cup.

8. Cut two one inch diameter circles from a colorful card.

9. Glue the other end of the string between the two circles with wrong sides together to make the ball.

Toss the ball into the cup! Have a contest and see who can catch the most balls in a minute.

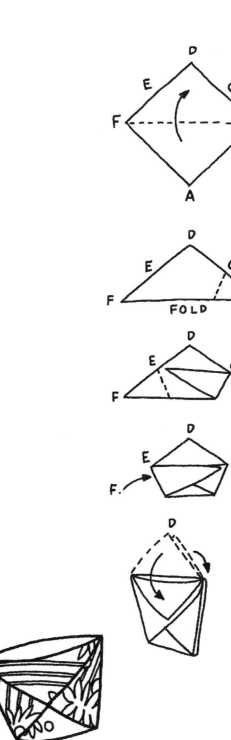

Jumping Jack

1. Use the pattern on page 46 to cut out Jumping Jack's head and body from a plain card or paper. Draw Jack's face and hair.

2. Cut out a vest, pants, and tie from colorful cards. Glue them on Jack's body.

3. Punch four holes in Jack's body as the pattern illustrates.

4. Cut out two arms and two legs from a plain card.

5. Cut pant legs and sleeves from colorful cards.

6. Glue sleeves to arms and pants to legs.

7. Punch two holes at the top of each arm and each leg.

8. Attach the arms and legs to the back of Jack's body with brad fasteners, leaving the end holes free in the arms and legs.

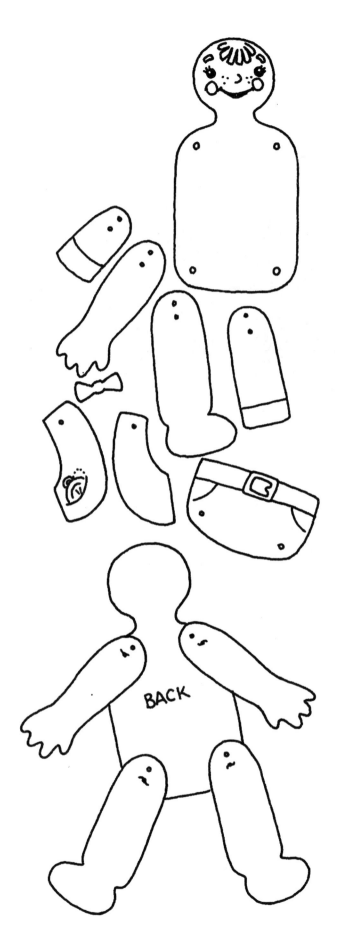

44

9. Lay Jack face down with arms and legs close to the body.

10. Thread a string through the two end holes in the legs and tie it together. Trim string.

11. Thread a string through the two end holes in the arms and tie it together. Trim string.

12. Tie a long string to the arm string and then the leg string as illustrated. Tie a bead to the end of the long string hanging down.

Hold Jack by the head and pull the string to see him jump.

Patterns

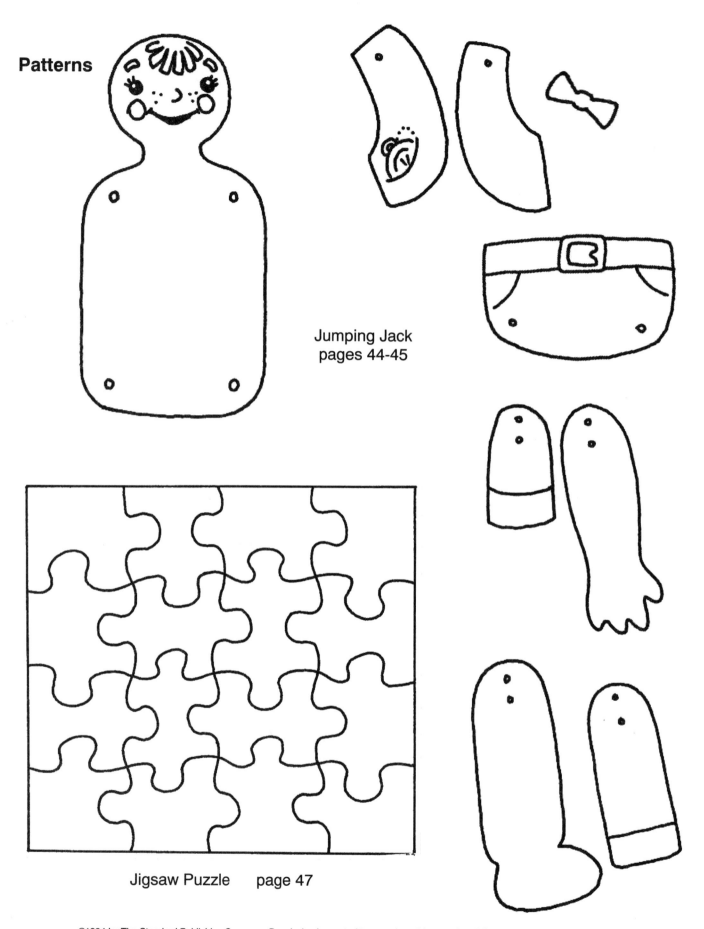

Jumping Jack
pages 44-45

Jigsaw Puzzle   page 47

Jigsaw Puzzles

1. Cut a card into puzzle pieces. (The pattern on page 46 may be used.)

2. Store each puzzle in a separate envelope.

   Trade a puzzle with a friend.

Sewing Card

1. Find a card with a large simple shape. Glue the front and back together to make the picture stiff.

2. Punch holes about every fourth inch around the shape.

3. Cut a piece of colorful yarn approximately twice the length of the outline of the shape. Dip the ends of the yarn in melted wax or wrap the ends with clear tape to make "sewing" easier.

Puppet Show

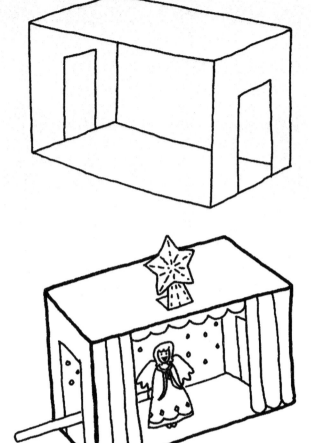

1. Stand a box such as a shoe box on its side horizontally. This will be the puppet stage.

2. Cut a vertical rectangle in both ends of the box. These will be the side doors to enter the puppets.

3. Add curtains to the stage front by cutting a large card in half and taping each to the box as in the diagram.

4. Cut characters from cards to tell a story such as the birth or death of Jesus. Glue each character on to a long strip cut from a card to make the puppets.

5. As the story is told, enter the puppets through the stage side doors.

Write a script and put on a show!

Paper Dolls

1. Trace paper doll patterns from page 50 onto a plain card. Cut out.

2. Lay each doll on the back of a colorful card and draw a costume a little larger than the doll. Draw tabs at various places to fasten the clothing onto the doll. Cut out.

3. Cut shoes, hair bows, etc. from scraps and glue to the dolls.

Create several costumes.

Patterns

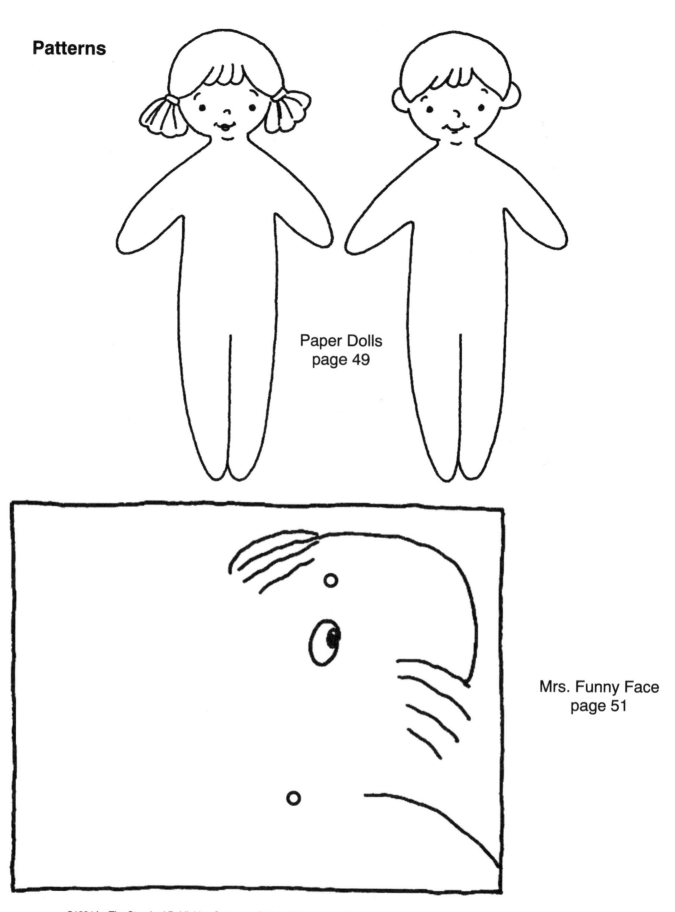

Paper Dolls
page 49

Mrs. Funny Face
page 51

Mrs. Funny Face

1. Trace the pattern on page 50 on to the plain side of a 4" x 5" card.

2. Punch two holes at the forehead and neck as in the illustration.

3. Insert each end of an 8-10 inch thin metal chain through a hole on the right side, and tape the ends to the wrong side.

4. Glue another card that has been trimmed to the same size to the back of the face to cover up the taped chain ends.

5. Cut a hat from a colorful card for Mrs. Funny Face. Cut out and glue on a flower for Mrs. Funny Face to smell with her chain nose. Draw in other details or decorate as you wish.

Arrange the chain in different ways to make funny faces.

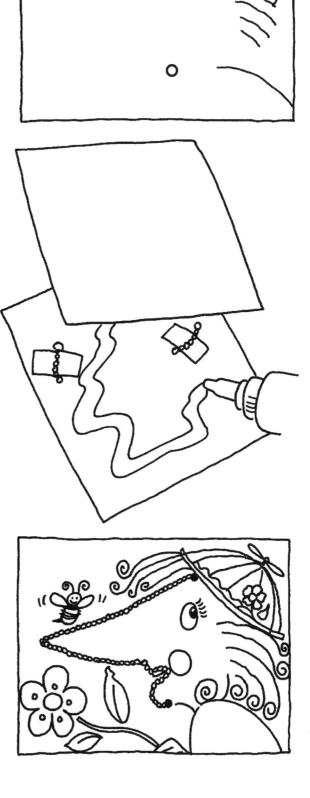

Peacock

1. Use two card fronts with wrong sides together and the pattern below to trace and cut out a peacock body.

2. Glue the cards together leaving the peacock's back open.

3. Choose 3-4 cards and trim all to the same size. Then glue together side by side with right sides up.

4. Pleat the shorter side from end to end.

5. Gather one side of the pleated strip and glue between cards in the peacock's back.

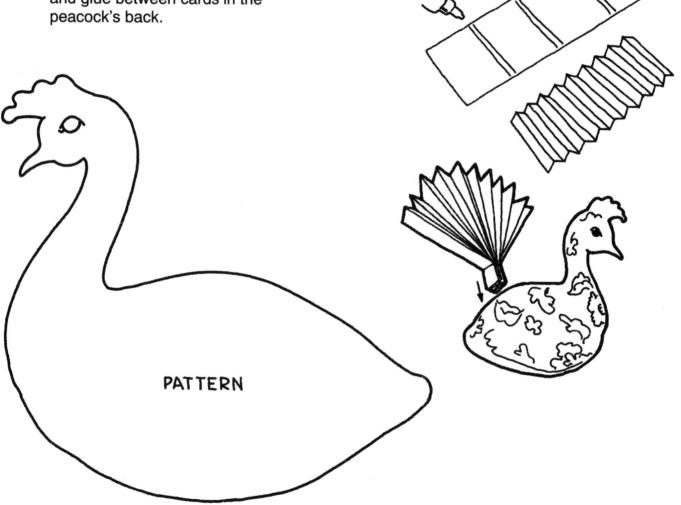

PATTERN

A Spinning Top
(Pictured on cover.)

1. Choose a colorful card and cut it into a 3" diameter circle.

2. Find the center of the circle and make a small hole.

3. Insert a sucker stick or a wooden kitchen match (with the head removed) through the hole. Secure with a drop of glue.

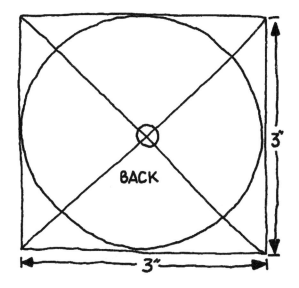

Have a contest and see whose top spins the longest.

Building Cards
(Pictured on cover.)

1. Make building cards three layers strong—a card, glued to its back which is glued to another card. Be sure that decorated sides face out on both sides.

2. Cut cards into 3" squares or larger.

3. Cut six slits into each card as in the diagram.

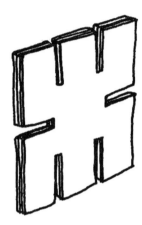

Slip building cards together to build a house or castle.
Or see who can build with the most cards before they fall.

People for Your Building

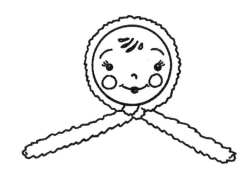

1. Draw a face on a small wood bead.

2. Wrap a chenille wire over the head and twist at the neck for hair. Spread the ends for arms.

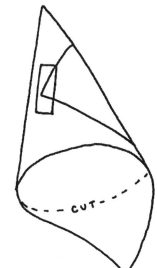

3. Make a small cone from a colorful card. Trim like the diagram.

4. Glue the head and arms to the cone.

Use bead dolls with your building (see page 54).

Fun With Secret Doors

1. Find a card with several small pictures.

2. Cut another card to the same size. Use an X-Acto® knife to cut doors in this card to align with the small pictures when laid on top of the first card.

3. Glue the card with cut doors to the top of the card with small pictures. Be careful not to glue the doors closed.

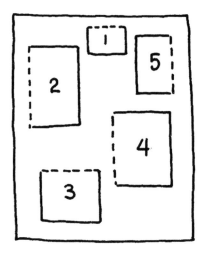

Write a message on the picture card, and cut a door for your message too. Give the card to a friend!

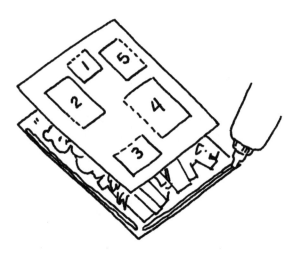

A Peek Box

1. Start with a rectangular box such as a shoe box. (The lid will not be used.) Decorate the outside as desired.

2. Cut an opening in one end of the box about 1" x 2".

3. Cut out animals, people, and any other objects from cards for your peek box scene. Leave about 1-2" of the card at the bottom of each object to fold back to use as a stand as illustrated in the diagram.

4. Choose a background card to glue inside the peek box.

5. Make paper springs to attach some objects to the background to make them 3-D.

   a. Cut cards into ½" wide strips.
   b. Tape or glue two equal length strips at right angles.
   c. Alternate folding one over the other until all the paper is folded.
   d. Tape or glue the end.

6. Glue cutouts to the floor of the box by staggering them so all are visible. Small objects should be near the background with large objects near to the peek hole.

7. Glue or tape a sheet of white tissue paper over the top (in place of the lid).

Peek at the picture!

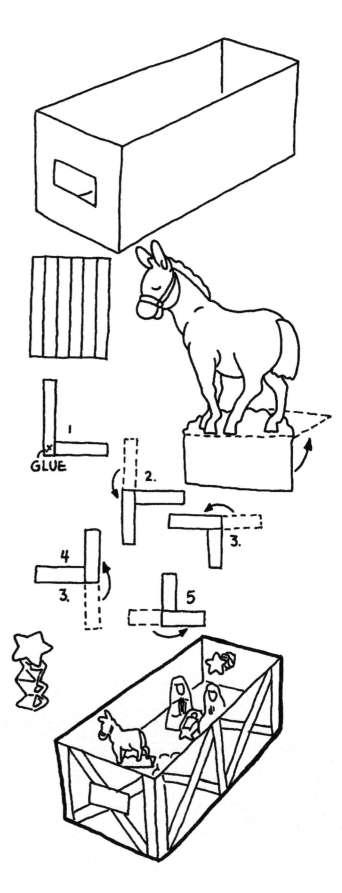

Marching Soldier

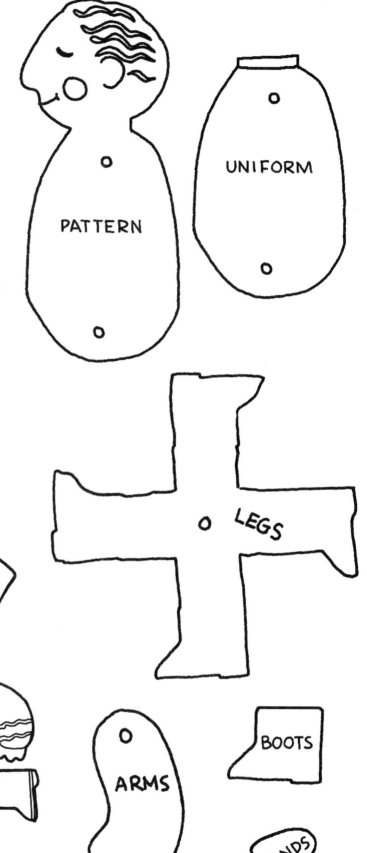

1. Trace the head and body profile onto a plain card. Cut out.

2. Use a colorful card to cut out two arms and a uniform. Glue the uniform to the body front.

3. Punch two holes in the body as illustrated.

4. Punch a hole in the top of the arms and fasten the arms (one on each side) to the upper body with a single brad fastener.

5. Cut two hands from a plain card and glue them at the end of the arms.

6. Cut legs from a colorful card. Punch a hole in the center.

7. Cut boots from a contrasting card and glue on to the legs.

8. Use a brad fastener to fasten the legs loosely to the lower back of the body.

Take your soldier for a march!

Christmas

Bell Ornament
(Pictured on cover.)

1. Fold four cards in half and cut four bells as shown in the diagram. Use the pattern below.

2. Fold each bell with the card front inside.

3. Cut a cord or piece of yarn three times the height of the bell. String on a metal jingle bell.

4. Glue the four card bells together on the back side with the folded cord between them.

5. Tie the cord together at the top.

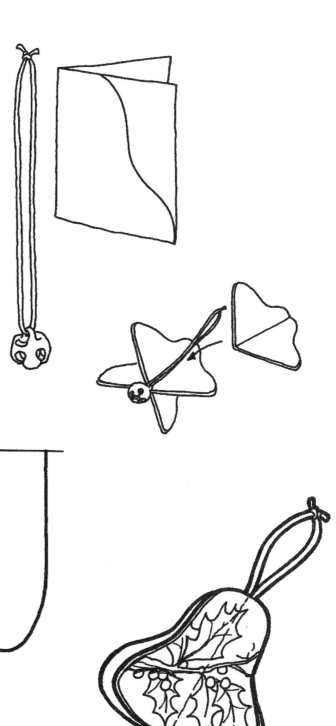

PATTERN

Hang bells on a Christmas tree or add to a package as a decoration that can later be used as an ornament.

Tree Ornament

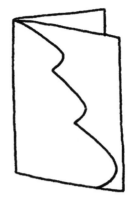

1. Fold four cards in half and cut four trees as shown in the diagram. Use the pattern below.

2. Fold each tree with the card front inside.

3. Glue the four trees together on the back side with a short piece of looped cord or ribbon between them at the top.

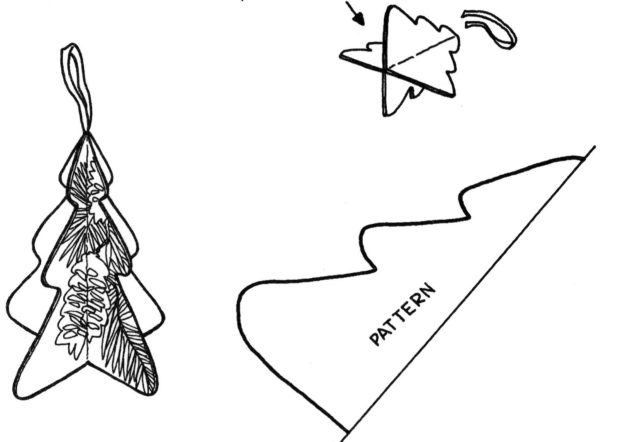

PATTERN

Hang trees from pegs or use them as party favors.

Sleigh

1. Cut two sleigh sides from two card fronts.

2. Cut a long 3" wide strip of plain card. Piece together if necessary.

3. With the wrong side of the strip facing up, fold in about a fourth inch on each side.

4. Glue or tape the folded edge of the strip (decorated side up) to first one plain side of the sleigh and then the other to make the floor of the sleigh. Snip folded edge at bends to shape more easily.

5. Punch two holes in the front of the sleigh. Tie in a cord or ribbon.

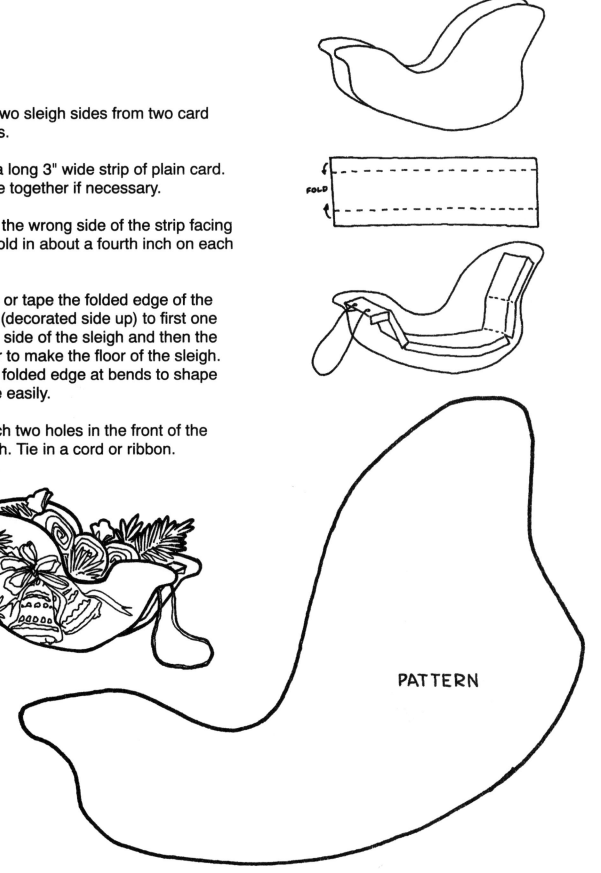

PATTERN

Use the sleigh as a table decoration, or fill it with candy.

Doily Ornament

1. Cut out pictures or shapes from cards.

2. Glue a card shape in the center of a paper doily.

3. Thread ribbon or cord through the doily to make a loop for hanging.

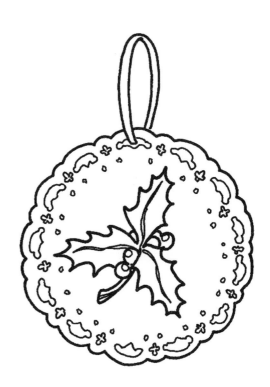

Cornucopia

1. Roll a card into a cone and secure it with tape.

2. Trim the top if desired.

3. Punch two holes at the open end. String in and tie a ribbon or yarn hanger.

Fill with candy, pencils, or anything. Hang cornucopias on the Christmas tree, or wrap them in clear plastic and give to a friend.

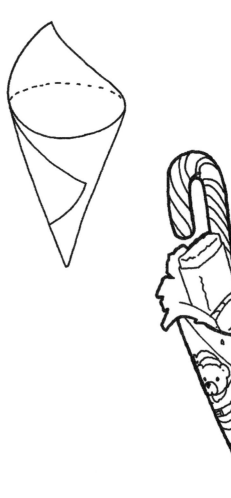

Simple Ornaments

1. Cut two cards into identical shapes with pictures facing out. Use patterns on page 64 or make your own.

2. Glue wrong sides together.

3. Punch a hole to add a yarn or cord hanger.

4. Add glitter if desired.

Clear glitter sprinkled lightly over the whole shape adds a special touch.

Patterns

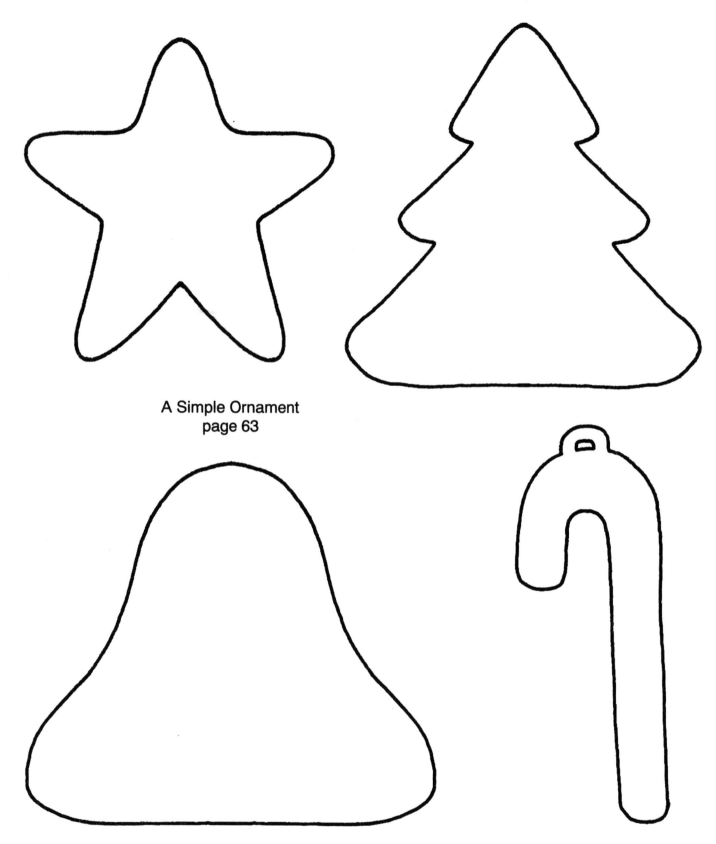

A Simple Ornament
page 63